EDUtainment
Entertainment in the K-12 Classroom

Bryan D. Svencer, M.Ed.

ISBN-13: 978-1479244676
ISBN-10: 1479244678

Dedicated to my loving and supportive wife, Tina, my little baby girl, Evangeline Grace, my family, my friends, my colleagues, my past professors, & all fellow teachers of the present/future.

EDUtainment /ˌejəˈtānmənt/ (n):

1 the byproduct of simultaneously educating and entertaining a student
2 an entertaining incentive that occurs in an educational setting
3 a philosophy and/or way of thinking that merges entertainment and education

Author's Note

The ideas and strategies in this book worked well based upon the contextual factors, needs, and interests of the students in my school. Every educator has a very unique and diverse teaching philosophy, comfort level, and teaching style. The accounts in this book are a part of my journey as an educator. Regardless of any teaching style, if implemented correctly, I am confident several or all of the strategies in this book can be altered to complement your teaching situation as well as bring joy to and enhance the learning experiences of your students.

Contents

Introduction

Although settling into your comfort zone may be tempting, it will not put you on the track to success. Growing personally and professionally requires you to bolster your risk-taking skills.[1]

-Jim McCormick, *professional skydiver & innovator*

Several years ago when I was an undergrad at Millersville University, I took an elective course entitled Geography of Europe to fill one of the required blocks to graduate. I was always fascinated by Europe and had heard that the professor was from London and had a great sense of humor. He was the kind of guy that you'd run into at a Doc Holliday's playing pool, which I did once, and had to assist him in picking up and moving a pool table, because the squirrely and immature undergrads playing next to him were getting in his way. I was one of the undergrads playing next to him. He picked up one side of the table with one hand and held a pint of beer in the other hand. I, of course, used both hands to assist him. I wouldn't want to suffer the consequences of spilling a beer on my professor's game table.

In his course, Geography of Europe, one of our assignments required us to write a paper on "anything" related to Europe. The gifted and dynamic professor was practical and knew that his students came to him from a wide range of majors and had a broad spectrum of interests. At the time, I was learning about Montessori schools, which originated in Rome, in an early childhood course that I was taking that same semester. I was fascinated by the non-traditional and hands-on approach of the Montessori Method.

I ran my idea for the paper past the professor, trying to explain the Montessori approach in as short amount of time as possible. (The professor was very witty and quick on his feet. You didn't want to engage in a conversation with him for very long in front of a class of forty students.) However, it was his wittiness and humor that spurred my idea to write this book. As I was explaining the

Montessori process, the professor rebutted with his English wit, "What is this? *EDUtainment?*" It was right then that it hit me. I thought, "Yeah. In this day and age children are bombarded with entertainment and technology. If we want to reach out to students and keep them engaged, especially elementary-aged students, we need to embrace the idea of *EDUtainment.*"

From that point on, I kept on that mindset of *EDUtaining* students. It is ironic, however, that a key part to my philosophy of education didn't come from a professor in the education department, but from a handsome, witty, portly young Brit from the geography department. It is a testament to show how much of an influence teachers can have on a student, even if it comes from only a thirty-second conversation.

Although the Montessori methods are very different from my own, it was the method's individuality that acted as a catalyst to inspire me to try some techniques of my own, silly as they may be.

Student testimonials:

I love your ways of mixing fun, silliness, and learning together!

The environment in our classroom is a nice place to be learning in.

Thanks for being an amazing teacher!

You are really good at teaching and at having fun. You are a one in a million teacher.

Thank you for turning fourth-grade around and making it an awesome dance party!

Thank you for making all of our subjects fun by making up vocab basketball, math basketball, and fun skits. You are the best!

You made learning enjoyable and fun!

Thanks for making everything fun. 4th grade was the greatest year I ever had. I was so happy to come to school everyday. Everyday was a great day for me.

The day I got to school I just knew that you were going to be the best teacher ever, and I was right about that. You are the nicest and funniest teacher in the whole wide world!

I hope your day is full of laughter…oh wait, every day with you is a day of laughter!

Mr. Svencer is a rock star!

Thank you for the best year ever!

Thank you for everything that you did to make fourth-grade a great year! I'm going to miss you a lot when I go to middle school!

You are so much fun coming up with so many games.

Mr. Svencer, thanks for being amazing at teaching.

My favorite thing about class was the disco ball and the basketball hoop!

Parent testimonials:

Thank you, Mr. Svencer, for providing a creative and fun classroom for learning. Thanks for making fourth-grade such a great year for Mason. You've made it so much fun that Mason doesn't want it to end. You obviously love teaching and enjoy the kids, which makes them love school. What a gift! You grip them. You will be one of those teachers Mason always remembers.

Although each teacher is loved, Mr. Svencer will never be forgotten for his disco snack.

He enjoyed having you as a teacher, especially all the fun things you incorporated into learning. I'm sure all the kids will be missing those disco snacks and light shows!

Joel enjoyed being in your class tremendously!

Just wanted to say "thank you" so much for being such a wonderful teacher to Eric!! He's had the best school year ever because of you!!

Thanks for making every school day fun! Evan adores you! You're an awesome teacher with so much patience, kindness, and understanding.

Thanks for a great year in fourth-grade. Brandon has truly enjoyed your class.

We all have memories of that special teacher - the one who made such a vivid impression on us that we remember his or her name for the rest of our lives. For Norah, that's you. When she's old like me she'll remember you for the way you made her laugh and taught her something totally new and fun each day she went to school. Not many kids can say that. I'm grateful beyond measure that she had that experience.

Your techniques held the interest of both my children and were effective in teaching the given curriculum. As an elementary reading specialist, M.Ed., I can say with full confidence that my children received a well-rounded education while in your class. Successfully educating children goes far beyond covering the curriculum. You accomplished this in a way that few teachers can.

Chapter Zero

Flashback

(A.K.A. Prior Knowledge for You)

Growing up as a child, I had always been a fan of lights, laser shows, and music. My bedroom as a kid displayed a rotating multicolored disco light set atop a stereo system. The back right corner of my room was home to a musical keyboard that boasted red illuminating keys. The keyboard acted much like a player piano. However, unlike a player piano, instead of the keys depressing as a chosen song was automatically being played, the keys would light up in red as each note was being played.

Besides the light and musical theme in my bedroom, an even more overpowering theme was EVERYTHING MICHAEL JORDAN. I had a life-sized cardboard cutout of Michael in the corner of my room opposite the keyboard corner. Aside of the life-sized cutout was a very large Michael Jordan hoop that would overtake the bedroom if it were any bigger. The walls were covered in Michael Jordan posters, framed and unframed, as well as other Michael Jordan memorabilia neatly displayed and preserved in clear plastic cases both on shelves and behind glass. I had collected Michael Jordan cologne, magazines, books, comic books, unopened figurines, and well-over 500 Michael Jordan cards well-preserved in transparent sleeves. Collecting Michael Jordan memorabilia was a pastime that one of the best men in my wedding, Greg, and I had shared, and it kept us out of trouble growing up…for the most part!

When I graduated from Millersville University and landed my first teaching job, I moved in with my future brother-in-law, Patrick, and his wife, Deanna, for a year. Instead of bombarding their home with all of my child-like possessions, I felt I needed to get creative. It was during those thoughts that I had a brilliant IDEA. I thought, "If I enjoyed many of the items in my room as a child and still enjoy them today, then certainly, my students will enjoy the items as well. And, I won't have to spend a ton of money purchasing decorations for my classroom."

I was going to be married within a year and needed to save up a lot of money for the wedding. At the time, I was having a hard time grappling with the idea of how expensive our wedding cake could possibly be. A cake that was fashioned with only twenty-five dollars worth of material could cost over $500! Seriously. Up to that point, I hadn't spent $500 or more on any single item, except for my car, of course, and now I was expected to spend that much on a cake!

Into my first year of teaching I strutted, a young man looking no older than the age of sixteen, carrying a disco-ball, stereo, light-up keyboard, large basketball hoop, and life-sized Michael Jordan cutout, among other things. I could just see my principal, Kristen, thinking, "I hope I made a good choice in hiring this guy."

As I strolled through the main office that summer, my principal looked at me like a young child would look at Pippi Longstocking, with wide-eyed amazement. She didn't know if I was going to be remarkable in a good way or a bad way and either did I. However, little did I know, all of the aforementioned items would play a pivotal role in who I would become as an *EDUtainer*, in addition to becoming the items many of my students would come to know and love.

Chapter One

DiscoSnack

*DiscoSnack is the best
thing you can possibly imagine!*
-4th grade student

When I was an elementary student, which wasn't many years ago, having a dance party during snack time was unheard of. Today, it has become a reality.

During my first week of teaching, I was informed by my teammates that most classrooms allowed a time for students to enjoy a snack. I thought, "Wow, what a great idea! Having a snack time will provide me with a few extra minutes to gather materials for my next lesson." However, little did I know that I would need a little "down-time" to refuel just as much as the kids.

During our first snack, one of my students asked me what the spinning ball of light hanging in the corner was for (see Figure 1), so I turned on the spinning ball of light, added some music, and we performed the popular party anthem known as the "Cha-Cha Slide" together during snack time.

Earlier in the day, we had performed the "Cha-Cha Slide" to get our wiggles out, and the students were requesting a Cha-Cha encore. It seemed appropriate to add the dance to our snack party.

One idea led to another. The lights went down. The disco light was spinning. My musical keyboard keys were flashing red. A projector was displaying a psychedelic screensaver onto a large white surface. And the kids were having the time of their lives.

As the week progressed, students could not stop talking about my newly coined term, DiscoSnack. During that week, a light bulb (figurative) went off in my new teacher mind. "I can utilize DiscoSnack as a reward for good behavior," sparked my cerebellum.

I wrote the letters R E S P E C T vertically on the board (No, I was not going to begin playing Aretha Franklin music!). I told the students that each time the majority of the class was caught not following one of our school rules, a letter would be removed from the word RESPECT. And if they still had at least one letter left by the last day of the week, then we would have DiscoSnack on Friday.

Unfortunately, when new ideas are being introduced, it takes a little adjusting to get things right. I was going to say "tweaking" but that is my least favorite "buzz" word in the field of education.

My heart was pounding faster than a puffed-up hammer slamming Whac-A-Moles at Chuck E. Cheese.

When DiscoSnack was in its early stages, we sometimes got complaints about noise from innocent bystanders walking by the room, as well as individuals from the room below who complained about hearing a banging noise. As a result, I quickly incorporated rules to avoid distracting other classrooms and students. The rules are outlined later in this chapter.

In my second week of teaching, during our first earned DiscoSnack, the principal walked into the room. Kids were dancing. Music was thumping. Lights were flashing. And, my heart was pounding faster than a puffed-up hammer slamming Whac-A-Moles at Chuck E. Cheese. I didn't know how the principal was going to react. Little did I know, however, she could bust a move better than Michael Jackson. Instead of asking the students what was going on, she began dancing along with us.

My principal's reaction reminded me of the time I displayed dancing badgers on a large surround-sound video system within a large lecture room at the university for which I was completing my undergrad work. When my handsome, witty, portly, young, and British geography professor walked in, he walked up to the podium, stopped, paused for a moment, and began bobbing his head in unison with the badgers on the screen. Ironically, as mentioned in my introduction, this particular professor was the one who helped coin the term *EDUtainment*. He was the biggest *EDUtainer* of them all.

Both my professor's and principal's unexpected reactions "kick-started" my confidence to continue on my path of *EDUtaining* students. From the day my principal danced with us, DiscoSnack has become legendary at my school.

Why bother?

A weekly classroom incentive like DiscoSnack decreases wasted class time by providing an objective and set of guidelines to place in motion a quick way to motivate students to remain on-task. As a result, I don't have to spend a great deal of time reprimanding children. If the majority of the class is off-task, I simply say the words, "Take away a letter," and everyone snaps back into line like a group of elitist band students in the Macy's Thanksgiving Day Parade. In reality, I gain hours of instruction Monday through Thursday by simply adding flare to ten to fifteen minutes of snack time on Friday.

Since my early DiscoSnack days, the fanfare has evolved to also include a laser light show, karaoke performances, and a flashing traffic light. I can't wait to see what DiscoSnack will look like the year I retire!

Suggestions:

⇒ Make sure none of your students placed a miniature carton of chocolate milk from lunch into his front jeans pocket. One of my students did this once, forgot he placed it there, and attempted to do the "worm" while the music was playing. Let's just say it didn't end well. Milk bomb. Creamy-sweet geyser. Wet pants.

⇒ You can never have too many lights, unless, of course, you have a student in your class that is susceptible to seizures.

⇒ Make sure the classroom door remains closed. If someone leaves the door open, end DiscoSnack immediately. You don't want to distract any other students in the school from learning. A swift and severe consequence will remind students to be more careful in the future.

⇒ Test for an appropriate volume level prior to the party.

⇒ Students should never participate in dancing with food in their mouths.

⇒ If students are performing the "Cha Cha Slide" or similar dance, instruct them to perform soft "marshmallow-like" jumps. Stomping should never be allowed if another classroom is below you.

⇒ Never leave DiscoSnack for a substitute to manage. I tried that once, and it didn't turn out so well for her! The substitute never returned to my room.

⇒ Never allow DiscoSnack to last longer than 15 minutes.

⇒ Don't joke about having a completely fictitious event known as CriscoDisco in front of your school nurse. She won't find your idea very amusing. (CriscoDisco would include a combination of dancing and eating lots of fatty foods.)

⇒ One can utilize DiscoSnack as a team incentive or individual incentive. I prefer to use DiscoSnack as a team incentive. As an individual incentive, I administer a daily behavioral grade to each student to help him or her work towards earning extra recess at the end of each week.

⇒ If you are a secondary teacher, you can incorporate DiscoSnack for 15 minutes at the end of each unit for students that handed all of their assignments in on time or acquired a certain letter grade, etc.

The Skinny:

Incorporate a weekly whole class incentive, like DiscoSnack, to decrease misbehavior and encourage students to follow the school and/or classroom rules throughout the week.

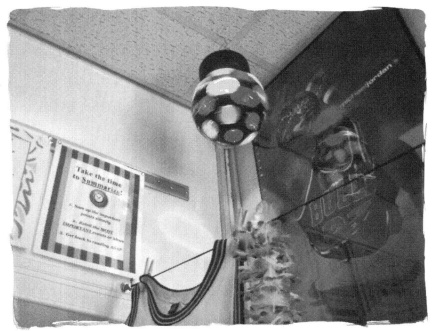

Figure 1: Spinning Ball of Light

Chapter Two

The Voice

Hey, you sound like the
Dunkin' Donuts worker by my house!
-4th grade student

Unsurprisingly, as each school year progresses, a teacher's voice begins to sound like the faint hum of a classroom fan. One can feel it blowing, but he/she has become so accustomed to the sound that he/she no longer notices the audible vibration. I had become a hum.

I was introducing a mind-numbing lesson on subjects and predicates one year, and my students were staring at me like a bunch of little yard gnomes. Their eyes were glued to my lips out of obligation, but I knew they weren't hearing a word I was saying.

> **I was introducing a mind-numbing lesson on subjects and predicates one year, and my students were staring at me like a bunch of little yard gnomes.**

I knew I had to do something, or my time would be wasted. So, I immediately started speaking in a fake Southern park ranger accent (see Figure 2).

"Howdy, partners! I'm Ranger Roy, and I'm here today to talk about subjects of a sentence. The 'subject of a sentence' is who or what the sentence is about…Yeeee hawww! Jake, would you like to be the 'subject' of a sentence?"

Suddenly, my students had become as attentive as a bunch of dogs begging for food. I had abruptly changed the tone of the lesson by introducing a new character into the room. Not only were my students *EDUtain*ed, but they all performed very well on their next quiz.

Since then, I've added a few additional accents to my repertoire and introduce the accents as needed. Accents can be a natural and effective A.D.D drug in the classroom. No lie. "The Voice" works miracles. Feel the healing power of "The Voice."

Why bother?

Students need a change of pace. Every school year, students get to a point where consistency becomes monotonous oblivity. Educators need to find a way to "mix things up" to promptly reel students back in. Teachers are responsible for teaching their school's required curriculum. If students aren't listening, then students aren't learning. Something as simple as a new accent can be the remedy.

Suggestions:

⇒ Please do not stay in character all school year. Pee-Wee Herman tried that once, and we all know how that turned out for him.

⇒ Improvise accents while teaching. Students will not know the difference. I've been known to change accents several times in a matter of seconds.

⇒ If you already sound like a Southern park ranger, try using a New York, Canadian, Boston, surfer dude, British, or Indian accent. My newest edition is a Valley Girl accent.

⇒ Never be afraid to introduce "The Voice." No prior acting experience is required or needed. Believe me, I've had neither. Unless of course, you consider being a mascot at Chuck E. Cheese acting experience.

⇒ If you are a secondary teacher, you can tailor your accent to coincide with your subject area. If you teach science, tailor your accent to that of a mad scientist. If you teach literature, tailor your accent to include Old English. If you teach math, tailor your accent to mimic a movie version of Albert Einstein. Explore the possibilities.

The Skinny:

Begin speaking in a fake accent when the majority of the class becomes disinterested to grab student interest and draw them back into the lesson.

Figure 2: The Voice

Chapter Three

Rock 'N' Rules

I think it is neat that famous people teach us the school rules!
It shows that everyone has to follow the rules!
-4th grade student

During my college years as an undergrad, I came to appreciate a Grammy Award-winning surfer rock band from San Diego named Switchfoot. Never in my wildest dreams did I imagine that they would someday assist me in creating a motivational video of my school's rules. However, they did just that!

Most of the members of Switchfoot are surfers. In fact, Switchfoot is actually a surfing term. In an interview, Jon Foreman, the lead singer, stated:

> We all love to surf and have been surfing all our lives so to us, the name made sense. To switch your feet means to take a new stance facing the opposite direction. It's about change and movement, a different way of approaching life and music.[1]

As an educator, I have always attempted to approach teaching in a way similar to how Switchfoot approaches life and music. As evident by the title of this book, since the very beginning, I've taken a different stance on how I approach teaching. Of all the rock bands in the world, it is fitting that Switchfoot would become a part of my journey as an educator. We each have similar philosophies of how we approach our careers. We don't fit a mold. We always think outside of the box and strive to do what's best for our fans and/or our students. Moreover, we both love what we do and feel we have the best jobs in the world.

BACK TO THE POINT:

I've talked to a lot of teachers that love to attend concerts, and there is sometimes talk of teachers acquiring backstage passes. I happen to be one of those teachers.

Several years into my teaching career, I acquired backstage passes to a Switchfoot concert. Once again, my cerebrum sparked an idea. I thought, "I can print our school rules on the back of our reward cards and have the members of the band recite the rules into my digital video recorder." At the time, I had taken up video editing as a hobby and was becoming pretty good at it. I knew once I got the footage I needed, I could create a video of a well-known band rocking out to our school's rules.

Students pay attention when rock stars have something to say!

I printed up the rules on the back of our reward cards, grabbed a bunch of T-shirts with our school logo on them to use as gifts, snatched up my camera, and headed off to the show. I couldn't wait for the meet 'n' greet session to begin. I was almost more excited to get the personalized video footage than I was to watch the actual show! Crazy! Sure enough, the band was more than willing to help out with the video, which was no surprise (see Figure 3). Chad, the drummer, introduced the band. Drew, the guitarist, spoke rule number one into the camera. Jon, the lead singer, guitar player, and songwriter, introduced rule number two. Romey, the keyboard player, shared rule number three. Lastly, Tim, the bassist, added his own words of wisdom. All members of the band spoke enthusiastically and added rock star swagger to their remarks. The band gratefully accepted the free school T-shirts as well! To say the guys in Switchfoot are the most sincere, humble, and nicest guys you could ever meet would be an understatement.

When I returned home, I edited the video, and our principal showed it at our first school-wide award assembly and continued to show it at numerous assemblies thereafter. Students and teachers loved the video. The viewings almost always resulted in students clapping along. Let's face it. Students pay attention when rock stars have something to say!

Since the creation of the video, I got the chance to share the film with the guys of Switchfoot, and it was well received by all of the members. My wife and I have both been blessed with numerous opportunities to hold various conversations with the band over the years. In some ways, they have become like family to us, and they are definitely the nicest and most selfless guys you'll ever meet. Some of their music was included in our wedding ceremony, and we had the opportunity to share the news of my wife's pregnancy with the lead singer before some of our family members and friends found out. (Those family members and friends shall remain unnamed.)

Why bother?

Using your backstage passes to get rock stars to review your school's rules will definitely capture students' interests and grab their attention. Because of the elevated interest, the rules will more easily remain in students' long-term memories, because they will likely want to watch the video over and over again. Repetition sticks.

How to Get a Star to Review Your School's Rules on Video:

⇒ Enter radio contests...even if you hate the band.

⇒ Obtain backstage passes to a rock show.

⇒ Print your school's rules onto portable cards.

⇒ Bring gifts.

⇒ Bring a video camera.

⇒ Kindly ask the "star(s)" to recite your school's rules into a video camera.

⇒ Find someone to help you edit the footage to create a sweet video, or edit the footage yourself.

⇒ If you are a secondary teacher, you can create a video that outlines your personalized classroom rules.

⇒ Go to **YouTube.com/EDUtainment23** to view my video entitled *Rock 'N' Rules feat. Switchfoot.*

The Skinny:

If you come across backstage passes to meet pop/rock/movie stars, kindly ask the "stars" to recite your school's rules into a video camera. Use the footage to create a rockin' video to showcase at assemblies and display on your school or classroom website, where my video resides.

Figure 3: Backstage with Switchfoot & Friends

Chapter Four

The Prop

*Why is there a banana
hanging from the ceiling?*
-4th grade student

A past professor of mine discussed the idea of using a prop to introduce a lesson. I gave his idea a try, and it worked like a charm.

Just prior to a school day when I planned on teaching a lesson on natural resources of the western region of the United States, I attached a banana from a white piece of string and hung the banana from the ceiling (see Figure 4). Enter "The Prop." No, I was not going to be teaching a sex ed. lesson to a bunch of 4th grade students.

From the moment my students entered the room, they kept asking, "Why is there a banana hanging from the ceiling?" I replied, "You'll just have to wait and find out." (I had peaked their interest all day long.) By not telling my students the prop's purpose right away, I had engaged their curiosity. Isn't that our goal as teachers? Don't we want students to be inquisitive and ask lots of questions? Props are a catalyst for curiosity.

Isn't that our goal as teachers? Don't we want our students to be inquisitive and ask lots of questions? Props are a catalyst for curiosity.

By the time we finally got to the lesson towards the end of the day, my students were so keyed up to having their curiosity satisfied, that they once again, were as attentive as a bunch of dogs begging for food. I gave them a nourishing meal. Figuratively, not literally. (No, I did not individually feed each student a bite of a vitamin-packed banana.)

We proceeded to identify the definition of a natural resource. Then, we had a valuable discussion about which U.S. regions were home to specific natural resources and how bananas were a natural resource of Hawaii. Furthermore, we discussed why natural resources are important to particular regions as well as how natural resources are useful to people.

In closing, it is important to note that a banana is arguably one of the most versatile and *EDUtaining* props available to an educator. And, the best part is, a banana can usually be purchased in most school cafeterias. Suggestion: Get a banana.

The Unparalleled Banana & Its Extraordinary Uses in the Modern Day Classroom:

Sample assignments in several subject areas:

LANGUAGE ARTS: Use adjectives and figurative language to describe a banana.

SCIENCE: Extract DNA from a banana and observe the DNA under a microscope.

FOREIGN LANGUAGE: Write a fictional story that includes a banana as the main character.

GEOGRAPHY: Label all of the areas of the world where bananas are grown.

HEALTH: Research the nutritional value of a banana.

PHYSICAL EDUCATION: Don't drop the banana relays.

MATH: Create a large coordinate plane and demonstrate translations, rotations, and reflections via a banana. Take a series of pictures to show each transformation.

THE ARTS: Sketch a banana that is residing in an odd location or use stop motion animation to create a short film that includes a banana as a character. One of my past students, Natalie Strickland, took it upon herself to create a stop motion animation project in 5th grade, entered it into a regional elementary school computer fair, and won first place! The video was entitled *Banana Peel's Dilemma!* Go figure.

Why bother?

An applicable prop will peak student inquisitiveness as well as give students a reference point to reflect upon, which will aid students in filing newly learned concepts into their long-term memories.

Suggestions:

⇒ Hang a basket at student eye level from the ceiling, and place a "Prop of the Day" in the basket each morning.

⇒ If you use a banana as a prop, don't let it rot. However, it does make the room smell like fresh banana bread during its early stages of rotting.

⇒ Make sure your prop is appropriate for your school setting.

The Skinny:

Incorporate the use of relevant props to peak student interest, trigger curiosity, and help students make connections to what they are learning.

Figure 4: The Prop

Chapter Five

Conference Call

Student to another student,
"That was the best lesson ever!"
-4th grade student

One day, as I was teaching a somewhat mundane lesson on mountains, my brain flashed with an idea. I thought, "We can call my college buddy, Gingy."

Gingy had become an OSHA worker in the mountains of Colorado after graduating college. His birth name is Brian Gingrich, but since I have a habit of giving people "hip-hop" names, I thought "Gingy" was appropriate. It has stuck ever since. (That's what it says in my phone contact list at least.)

The kids were astounded and *EDUtained.*

On a whim, I immediately turned the speakerphone component of my cell phone on, hooked the phone up to my computer speakers (see Figure 5), and dialed Gingy's number from my contact list. My students looked at me like I was crazy. I could just see them thinking, "What is he up to now?"

The phone rang a few times, and luckily, a voice spoke, "Bryan, is that you?"

I rebutted, "Hi, Mr. Gingrich! This is Bryan....uh, Mr. Svencer. I'm on the line with my fourth-grade students. We are learning about mountains. Would you be willing to answer some of their questions?"

"Really! Your whole class is on the line?" responded Gingy.

"Yes," I stated.

He couldn't back down now!

My students then proceeded to ask Mr. Gingrich lots of valuable questions about the wildlife, climate, plant life, culture, jobs, and natural resources found in the mountains of Colorado. Gingy, being the great guy that he is, proceeded to answer all of their questions. He even emailed us pictures of the wildlife, landforms, and plant life that could be seen from his front porch. The kids were astounded and *EDUtain*ed!

Of course, I didn't let him get off the phone without him telling the students some school-appropriate stories about his experiences in the Colorado Mountains. Gingy is a great storyteller, and strange things always seem to happen to him. You know the type.

Why bother?

Calling an expert in the field of what is being taught makes learning more real, fun, and relevant for students. Students learn by association and making a conference call gives students an opportunity to interact with a knowledgeable professional.

Suggestions:

⇒ I recommend setting up an appointment with your expert prior to calling him/her. I got very lucky my first time around. Hopefully, Gingy's boss didn't mind having Gingy involved in a thirty-minute phone conversation while he was on the clock.

⇒ If you decide to ignore my first suggestion and call someone on a whim, make sure they aren't the kind of person that answers the phone with profanity, "Hey buddy, how the !*$# are you?"

⇒ Ask your students to write down some questions onto a note card prior to the phone call.

⇒ Have your students write thank you cards to the expert and/or have them sing "Happy Birthday" to him/her on the appropriate day.

The Skinny:

Hold a student-led conference call with an expert related to what is being taught to help students make a real-world connection to what is being learned.

Figure 5: Conference Call

Chapter Six

Take Your Friend to Dance Day

Can you maybe come to my dance class on Saturday?
It is take your friend to dance day.
-4th grade student

During my first year of teaching, one of my students, Savannah Pukanccz, invited me to participate in her dance class at 8AM on a Saturday morning. She called it "Take Your Friend to Dance Day." I didn't want to let her down, so I conceded to her request. At the time, I hadn't previously been waking up prior to 10AM on a Saturday morning, but I bit the bullet. I figured I could go watch kids dance for an hour or so and be on my way. My prediction proved to be incorrect.

When I arrived at 7:55AM no student or parent was in sight. It was just the dance instructor and myself. We exchanged glances once or twice until she asked who I was. I proceeded to tell her my situation, at which she chuckled.

The instructor stated, "I think you might be the only guest joining the girls today!"

"Joining?" I asked. "I was under the impression that I would be observing."

"Oh no," the instructor stated. "Guests must participate."

I was screwed.

As she was finishing her sentence, a bunch of girls and parents came barging in through the front door like a swarm of crazy shoppers on Black Friday. The place was like a ghost town one minute and an amusement park the next.

Before I could sneak out the back door, my student and her

parents had spotted me. They laughed about my misinterpretation of the invitation and insisted that I participate. For some reason, I gave in to their request. To make things worse, I was the only "friend" in attendance that day and the only male dancer on the dance floor.

The session began with some easy stretches, which I could handle. Of course, I felt like a pedophile, however. Think about it. I was a man in my early twenties skipping around with a bunch of little girls.

As we were stretching, I noticed that Savannah's father had disappeared from behind the viewing glass. A few minutes later, he was back with a video recorder. His wife was taking pictures (see Figure 6), while he was taking video. Seriously? At the same time, the room full of mommies were declaring, "Awwww."

> I made my student's and her parents' day, and I taught my student a lesson in perseverance.

I felt like an idiot.

I had to gallop, prance, lift my leg, and leap like a female version of Air Jordan. During one leap my right pant leg got caught on my right heel, and I ripped my favorite pair of jeans up the leg. Everyone laughed, and I had to forge onward through another 30 minutes of dancing with my pants flapping in the wind like a denim flag.

In the end, everything turned out fine. I made my student's and her parents' day, and I taught my student a lesson in perseverance. Savannah could see that I was struggling through some of the routines, especially with my ripped jeans, but I never quit.

Pictures from the class ended up in my Christmas card from the family. Luckily, video footage from the event never surfaced onto the Internet. For that I am grateful.

Why bother?

Attending a student's dance class on a Saturday morning shows him/her that you care about him/her as a whole and wish to see him/her succeed at all aspects of life. It shows that you support him/her in being a well-rounded person and assists parents in reinforcing what they are trying to teach their child at home. In my particular case, I was able to take advantage of a "teachable moment" that taught my student about perseverance, starting what you finish, and making the best of any situation. Furthermore, the girls in the class were highly *EDUtain*ed.

Attending a student's extracurricular activities can also be a lesson in character education and generosity. Sadly, some students don't have parents that can attend their events. You may be the only one available to let them know you believe in them.

Suggestions:

⇒ Be selfless during unpaid off-school hours and attend a student's extracurricular activity at least once per school year.

⇒ Don't wear your favorite pair of jeans to a dance session.

⇒ Avoid pictures or video if you are dancing.

The Skinny:

Take some time out of your day to occasionally attend one of your student's extracurricular activities to build student rapport and teach a lesson in character education. Be prepared for anything and persevere. Take advantage of "teachable moments."

Figure 6: Take Your Friend to Dance Day

Chapter Seven

The Cardboard Assistant

*The cardboard assistant is very helpful! It lets you know the rules, so you
don't have to interrupt Mr. Svencer when he's with another reading group.*
-4th grade student

During my first year of teaching, I was put in charge of over twenty
students, and I was completely on my own with no teaching
assistant and no cooperating teacher. I was expected to be in
complete control of all of the kids. Even during my first job as a
game room attendant and mascot at Chuck E. Cheese, I was
provided with a group of team members to provide assistance in the
event the patrons decided to declare war against me. I needed an
assistant badly! Enter my life-sized Michael Jordan cutout (see
Figure 7). The Michael Jordan cutout that once resided in my
teenage bedroom had come to reside in my classroom and evolved
into my *EDUtaining* assistant and occasional dance partner during
DiscoSnack!

If I want my students to remember something important, say an
upcoming test or their math materials, I bring MJ to the front of the
room and pin the information to him. That guy has been poked,
pricked and jabbed more times than a teacher assigned to an
emotional support classroom.

MJ has helped me several times throughout my career. For
example, when students constantly ask me, "What do I need to take
to math?" I simply point to the 6 foot 6 inch tall guy standing at the
front of the room with the "math materials list" pinned to him, and
I move on to the next question. While writing this chapter, MJ had
the rules for center work pinned to him. I can honestly say that

centers have been running much smoother since MJ has been available to remind the students of how they are to act.

On a less serious note, I also like to strategically place MJ in front of the door just prior to the time the night custodian enters. Of course, MJ never fails to scare the "mop" out of him at each meeting, which helps build comradery around the workplace. (To get me back, he later installed a fart machine under my desk as well as programmed a universal remote to secretly turn on and change the television in my classroom when I wasn't looking.) MJ has instigated a number of pranks over the years, which has helped me build a rapport with my colleagues and the custodians in my building. And, any educator knows that the school custodian can be a teacher's best friend or worst enemy. Luckily, Michael Jordan has brought us together in a positive way.

The Michael Jordan cutout that once resided in my teenage bedroom had come to reside in my classroom and evolved into my *EDUtaining* assistant and occasional dance partner during DiscoSnack!

Why bother?

Jonathan Chase, one of the teachers I work with, refers to the act of students constantly wandering up to the teacher to ask a question or make a comment as "zombieing." Based upon my experiences as an educator, every teacher is a victim of "zombieing." Incorporating a cardboard assistant into the classroom provides teachers with an outlet to direct a student toward when he/she inevitably has a question in regards to common classroom practices and routines.

As mentioned previously, I pin center rules and expectations, among other things, onto our classroom's cardboard assistant. When a student "zombies" up to me as I am engaged with a guided reading group, I simply point to the cardboard assistant as a point of reference for the student. Nine times out of ten, the student consults with the cardboard assistant and returns to his/her seat. As a result, the students in my guided reading group are not interrupted and valuable discussion time is not wasted. Cardboard assistants decrease wasted class time.

Suggestions:

⇒ Never leave the cardboard assistant alone with the kids.

⇒ Find a cardboard assistant that you don't mind looking at or having "stand at attention" every day of your teaching career.

⇒ Don't overcrowd the cardboard assistant. Only pin him/her with the essentials.

⇒ Cardboard assistants can be found in attics, at yard sales, and on *craigslist*.

⇒ Don't be afraid to move the cardboard assistant around the room throughout the day.

⇒ Never resist your temptation to make the cardboard assistant dance.

⇒ Secondary teachers can post upcoming assignments and due dates on the cardboard assistant.

The Skinny:

Pin important information to a mobile life-sized cardboard cutout of your favorite celebrity. Students can use the cutout as a reference point to answer their most commonly asked questions. The cutout not only minimizes "zombieing" but becomes a room mascot and walking bulletin board.

Figure 7: Cardboard Cutout

Chapter Eight

Virtual Field Trips

That was hilarious!
-4th grade student

Many teachers have the opportunity to go on vacations with their friends and/or families, and most teachers own a camera with digital photo and video recording capabilities. In the course of my time as a teacher, I have had the opportunity to travel to Orlando, Florida and San Diego, California during my summer breaks. In Orlando, I visited Disney World and its surrounding area (see Figure 8). In San Diego, I kayaked in the Pacific Ocean, explored the world famous San Diego Zoo, took a safari at the San Diego Zoo Safari Park, boogie boarded with some surfers, etc.

A student fan favorite shows a scene of me screaming like a 10 year-old girl on a rollercoaster ride.

Both places provided me with many opportunities to gather video footage of the wildlife, plant life, culture, and history of each location. Consequently, I was able to utilize my editing skills to create an *EDUtaining* video for each locale.

As a fourth-grade teacher in Pennsylvania, I teach regions of the United States. When I am teaching "The South," I have the opportunity to take my students on a virtual field trip to Orlando, Florida. Similarly, when I teach "The West," I have the opportunity to take my students on a virtual field trip to San Diego, California. A student fan favorite shows a scene of me screaming like a 10 year-old girl on a rollercoaster ride. Let's just say I have a hard time following the rollercoaster rule: "Please No Video or Photography while Riding."

Why bother?

Most people take photographs and/or video while on vacation. It is very likely that some of the footage relates to your school curriculum. If you exploit the footage during a lesson, it is probable that students will take a high interest in what you are teaching. Who doesn't like looking at vacation pictures? Sharing personal experiences with students also helps to build a healthy rapport with students.

Suggestions:

⇒ Edit out profane language.
⇒ If you wear a bathing suit and/or drink alcohol while on vacation, do not include bathing suit and/or alcohol footage in your virtual field trip creation.
⇒ Only include embarrassing scenes if you don't mind a little student harassment.

The Skinny:

Utilize personal vacation videos and/or photographs to create a cost-effective and curriculum-based virtual field trip for students, which will build student rapport and assist learners in making real-world connections to what is being taught.

Figure 8: A Rhino at Disney's Animal Kingdom

Chapter Nine

Style:
Incorporating Pop Culture Into Your Lessons

I love your ways of mixing fun, sillyness, and learning together!
-4th grade student

Incorporating pop culture into your lessons is a great way to *EDUtain* students. One overwhelming morning, I was trying to think of an attention grabbing way to help students write with style, which happens to be one of the standards that I am required to teach in my district. Once again, my cerebrum sparked an idea.

I posted a picture of the latest female teen sensation onto my whiteboard. Her hair was up in a ponytail. She was wearing sweats. Her face was absent of makeup, and an iced coffee was clenched in her one hand while a shopping cart was clenched in her other. The class consensus was that Miss Sensation was not looking very stylish. I then proceeded to tell students that style is not needed when grocery shopping or writing a grocery list;

I also couldn't resist the temptation to show students how stylish I looked in a sport coat.

however, they agreed that style was needed in formal writing and at formal events like the Grammy Awards.

As a segway, I displayed a very stylish photograph of the same teen sensation in her red carpet dress and proceeded to ask students what steps she had taken to change her appearance. They stated that she had let down her hair, added some jewelry and make-up, and threw on a dress. We then conferred that fairly simple steps can be taken to add style to writing, just like simple steps can be taken to add style to one's appearance (see Figure 9). We discussed that colorful adjectives, attention-getting leads, and figurative language can be added to one's writing, while repetitive beginnings, unfocused sentences, and unneeded details could be removed. (I also couldn't resist the temptation to show students how stylish I looked in a sport coat).

To this day, students can recall how to add style to their writing as quickly as a bear defending her cubs.

Why bother?

Incorporating pop culture into a lesson helps students make connections to what they are learning and grabs student interest.

Suggestions:

⇒ Watch the Disney Channel and visit www.seventeen.com a couple of times a year to stay up-to-date on the latest teen sensations.

⇒ Relate icons of the past to icons of the present.

⇒ Avoid shady characters.

The Skinny:

Incorporate pop culture into your lessons to help students make connections to what is being taught.

Figure 9: Style

Chapter Ten

Hoop Dreams

*Vocabulary basketball is a fun and
exciting way to learn our new vocab. words!*
-4th grade student

A group of students stand in a straight line. A large stand-alone Michael Jordan basketball hoop rests four feet from the student at the front of the line. The teacher tosses the student a ball with numbers written all over it. The student looks down to see what numbers his/her thumbs land on. The student multiplics thc "thumbed" numbers together. If the student multiplies the numbers together correctly, he/she takes a shot. If the student makes the shot, he/she proceeds to the back of the line to continue game play. If a student multiplies the "thumbed" numbers together incorrectly, talks above a whisper, or misses the shot, he/she is eliminated. The game continues until there is one boy/girl standing. The winner receives a prize!

The above scenario is known as Math Basketball in my classroom. It makes learning fun, and once dangled in front of the students, it can then be used as an *EDUtaining* incentive. I personally use the game as a weekly incentive.

At the beginning of the week, I write the letters M A T H on my whiteboard. I then proceed to remove a letter from the word when the majority of my math class is not following our school rules. If there is at least one letter remaining on the whiteboard by the end of math time on Friday, we play Math Basketball for 10 minutes! Kids love it and work hard to earn game play! The best part is, they learn as well!

As I was setting up my classroom two weeks prior to the launch of my first year of teaching, a reporter from a local newspaper walked in and approached me to conduct an interview. My idea for the game was so well received that she featured it in a local newspaper story subtitled "Beach balls and cowboy hats encourage participation."[1]

Another hoop game we like to play in my classroom is known as Vocabulary Basketball. My language arts series incorporates a set of vocabulary words for teachers to introduce prior to each weekly lesson. At the beginning of each lesson, I assist my students in coming up with synonyms for each vocabulary word. I then display the words with their corresponding synonyms on the board. Students then proceed to line up and call out a vocabulary word with its corresponding synonym just prior to taking a shot. Vocabulary basketball is played in a similar fashion to math basketball in that if a student makes a shot after proclaiming a vocabulary word with its corresponding synonym, he/she proceeds to the back of the line to continue game play. If a student announces an incorrect meaning for a vocabulary word, talks above a whisper, or misses a shot, he/she is eliminated. Once again, the game continues until there is one boy/girl standing. The winner receives a prize! In my classroom, Vocabulary Basketball is even more popular than Math Basketball.

Kids love it and work hard to earn game play!

Another option for playing Vocabulary Basketball is to have each student choose a vocabulary word that he/she must utilize correctly in a sentence just prior to taking a shot. This option forces students to apply their knowledge of a word's meaning to create a sentence. This alternative is great for a second round of Vocabulary Basketball and forces students to listen to created sentences from their peers. Students hear the words being used in a variety of ways, which helps them gain a better understanding of each word's meaning.

Why bother?

Incorporating concept basketball into your classroom makes learning fun and gets students moving. Movement and a "change of pace" are beneficial for students of all ages. Research shows that games are motivating for students and movement increases brain function. Furthermore, concept basketball can be altered to be advantageous in almost every teaching situation.

Suggestions:

⇒ If you decide to store the hoop on top of a desk for added height (see Figure 10), make sure the hoop is secure. You don't want it to fall on a student!

⇒ Don't be afraid to show off your basketball skills in front of your students. You may not be Michael Jordan in real life, but it doesn't mean you can't be Michael Jordan in the classroom.

⇒ Plastic stand-alone play hoops can be found at garage sales, in department stores, or on *craigslist*.

⇒ K-2 teachers can have students identify a letter, number, or word prior to taking a shot.

⇒ Secondary teachers do not need to limit concept basketball to just vocabulary words and math facts. The possibilities are endless.

The Skinny:

Utilize a basketball hoop to incorporate concept basketball into your lessons. Concept basketball makes learning fun and gets students moving.

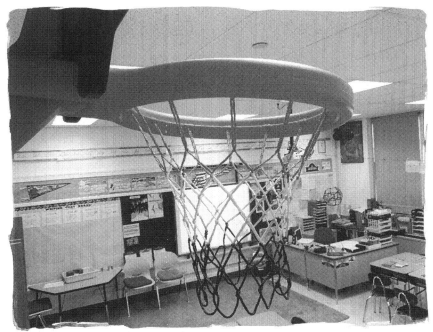

Figure 10: Hoop Dreams

Chapter Eleven

Karaoke Choreography

The line dance is a good way to remember things more challenging to remember.
I still remember most of the song! It helps a lot!
-5th grade student

While I was planning for a math lesson one evening, I came across a website entitled *StudyJams*. The site boasts an array of modern sounding karaoke songs that help explain a wide array of math and science concepts. *StudyJams* also hosts a variety of *EDUtaining* videos, slideshows, and step-by-step problems. It seems that the site is a big advocate of *EDUtaining* students.

One particular song that my students took a liking to was entitled "Types of Lines." The song has a Green Day meets Blink-182 kind of feel to it. The song's lyrical content outlines the definitions for vertical, horizontal, intersecting, parallel, and perpendicular lines. The chorus is as follows:

Horizontal lines – straight left and right
Vertical lines – up and down to the sky
Intersecting lines – cross all the time
Parallel lines – never touch the other lines
Perpendicular lines – intersect at right angles[1]

To have students demonstrate horizontal lines, I had them hold their right and left arms straight out from their sides. For vertical lines, I had students jump up and down like a rock star while pointing upward with a "fist pumping" motion. To showcase intersecting lines, I simply had students cross their arms in front of their chests. To demonstrate parallel lines, I had students place their right arms four inches above their left arms, horizontally in front of their chests. And, to show perpendicular lines I had students cross their arms at right angles in front of their chests. We practiced the motions a few times (see Figure 11) while I blasted the music over my computer speakers as the karaoke lyrics simultaneously scrolled across my interactive whiteboard along with my famous disco ball spinning overhead.

Suddenly, and without notice, my principal walked in.

My students proclaimed with echoing excitement, "Can we show Mrs. Campbell the line dance? Can we show Mrs. Campbell the line dance?"

I asked if she was interested in viewing our karaoke choreography, and of course she agreed. We proceeded to show her our performance, and it was a hit! In fact, this was the type of lesson where everything in the universe seemed to align and flow well together. Kids were learning. Kids were moving. Kids were having fun. This was the type of lesson creative teachers have on a weekly basis and hope an administrator will walk in to observe; however, it seems that administrators never show up for the great lessons, but usually end up "popping in" during a transitional time, test/quiz, or mundane type of lesson. In spite of all this, today was not that day!

When I checked my email at the end of the day, this encouraging message with "Thank you" written in the subject line was waiting for me:

> I'm reading a book entitled <u>What Great Teachers Do Differently</u>, and the title of the first chapter is, "It's About People, Not Programs." As I sat in your math lesson today, you brought this chapter to life for me. The "studyjams"

We practiced the motions a few times while I blasted the music over my computer speakers as the karaoke lyrics simultaneously scrolled across my interactive whiteboard along with my famous disco ball spinning overhead.

website is an incredible one, and the cooperative learning strategies (think-pair-share and math buddies) are also very powerful. However, both the technology and cooperative learning are effective in terms of making a difference in student learning because of YOU. You're really "a natural," and I admire your efforts to truly engage your students in learning.

Thanks,
Kristen[2]

My principal embraced the idea of *EDUtainment*! It was then that I thought, "An administrator that takes the time to concern herself with what is occurring in the classroom, reads books related to education, and gives feedback in an encouraging way makes a HUGE difference in student learning as well!" I was ecstatic and felt so blessed to be a part of such a cooperative and supportive school family.

Why bother?

Getting students moving and involved in the education process is very beneficial to their learning. Movement, motion, music, and scrolling lyrics can provide teachers with an opportunity to reach out to all learning styles and gives students a point of reference to reflect upon for recalling sought after information. During my experiences as a teacher, I have found that presenting information in song form also increases a student's ability to memorize new information more quickly than if he/she were to simply read the information over and over again on paper. It is important to note that memorization should not be the focus of any classroom. Problem solving, teamwork, respect, cooperation, safety, follow through, and work ethic should be a priority in the classroom; however, memorization has its place as well.

Suggestions:

⇒ Never incorporate motions that could be mistaken as obscene gestures.

⇒ If you are teaching older students, choose educational songs that include relevant/modern sounding beats and melodies. The following websites may be helpful.

- o www.StudyJams.com
- o http://flocabulary.com
- o www.TeacherTube.com
- o http://havefunteaching.com

⇒ As a Project Based Learning activity, encourage students to create their own songs and motions via free programs like iMovie in combination with GarageBand or Audacity in combination with Windows Movie Maker.

⇒ Record students performing karaoke choreography and post the videos on your school's website for all to enjoy.

⇒ The video entitled ***Karaoke Choreography "Types of Lines"*** can be viewed at **YouTube.com/EDUtainment23**.

The Skinny:

Incorporate educational karaoke and movement into your lessons to make learning fun and help students memorize facts efficiently.

Figure 11: Karaoke Choreography

Chapter Twelve

Step Up to the Microphone

Using the microphone is awesome!
Everybody hears you, and it is fun to use!
-4th grade student

You know the type. Shy. Quiet. When they speak, their voices are fainter than the hum of a refrigerator. They are almost mute. All teachers experience this type of student. We refer to them as desk gnomes. Everyone has different personality traits, and teachers must embrace all students; however, we must give every student the opportunity to be heard. We must do everything in our power to break desk gnomes out of their porcelain shells and give them voices. We must give them the chance to step up to the microphone.

When my sister returned from college one year, she was going through her unwanted possessions and asked if I wanted to keep her portable karaoke machine. I immediately thought, "This could be the answer to the desk gnome dilemma," and happily took the item off of her hands.

I took the device to school the next day, turned it on, sat it next to my desk (see Figure 12), and waited for the right opportunity to use it. Sure enough, after about fifteen minutes into the school day, I randomly chose a name stick to have a student share her journal entry. When she started reading, a few kids raised their hands and declared, "I can't hear her." I waved my hand in an inviting way towards the desk gnome and motioned to have her come towards my desk. I then spoke these five helpful words: "Step up to the microphone." I nicely requested that she read her journal entry into the microphone that was attached to the karaoke machine adjacent to my desk. She responded with a hesitant smile and was apprehensive at first but accepted my invitation. Once she started reading, it was as if we were at a rock show for writers. Finally, we could hear her beautiful voice and enjoy her superb writing. When she finished reading, all of the students cheered and affirmed her of what a great job she had done on her entry. I had unleashed a spark inside of her, and she has never looked back. From that point on, most everyone wanted a chance to use the microphone.

> **Once she started reading, it was as if we were at a rock show for writers.**

The karaoke machine has evolved to prove beneficial in several other ways:

1. As an incentive, students use the karaoke machine to sing their favorite songs during DiscoSnack.
2. Students use the karaoke machine when presenting projects with a partner.
3. The narrator uses the karaoke machine during reader's theater.
4. Teachers use the karaoke machine to make important announcements.

Why bother?

A portable karaoke machine is a fun way to make it easier for everyone to hear what is being spoken. And, most students embrace the opportunity to perform on stage. Every kid wants to be a star.

Suggestions:

⇒ Shop around to find an inexpensive karaoke machine with portability.

⇒ Use discretion when asking certain students to use the karaoke machine. You don't want to create a devastating experience for anyone and/or cause an anxiety attack.

⇒ Don't overuse the karaoke machine. If utilized too much,

students will become numb to this beneficial tool, and it will lose its effectiveness. However, if you are a teacher with a naturally quiet tone of voice or strained vocal chords, consider utilizing a wireless microphone while teaching. My school's physical education teacher has had great success with a wireless mic.

The Skinny:

Integrate a karaoke machine into a variety of classroom routines to amplify speech, improve student confidence, and boost classroom morale.

Figure 12: Karaoke Machine

Chapter Thirteen

Funkadelic Athletic Swag

The playground video with Mr. Svencer and Mr. Barndt
was so funny! They were wearing knee socks and sweatbands!!
-4th grade student

During my second year of teaching, my school's generous PTO raised enough money to purchase the school new playground equipment. After the equipment was installed, the physical education teacher asked a fellow teacher buddy, Mr. Barndt, and myself to show off our acting skills in a film entitled "Playground Safety." We gladly obliged.

On the way to our filming session we strutted out arm-in-arm wearing striped knee-high socks, rec-specs, headbands, armbands, athletic shorts, and T-shirts with our school logo printed on them. The two of us looked like we were transported directly from the *1970s*, but we knew the students would be highly *EDUtain*ed with the end result, so we pressed onward.

The phys. ed. teacher, Kliney, and a high school librarian, Maley, produced and directed the film. During filming, Mr. Barndt and I were instructed to climb the rope ladder, scale the infinity loop, stroll across the bridge, swing on the monkey bars, and struggle down the spiral slides. Our adult-sized legs got wedged between the opposite sides of the slides, so we looked like a bunch of tractor-trailers trying to round the corner of a school hallway. To make the filming procedure even more entertaining, the two of us incessantly gave each other high-fives and chest bumps throughout the entire process. We indisputably looked like a bunch of over-enthusiastic circus clowns.

The video made its debut at a school-wide assembly to commemorate the grand opening of the new playground equipment. After extensive editing, Maley was able to create a cohesive video that superbly outlined the "Do's & Don'ts" for Lincoln's new playground equipment. The video was very well received by both students and faculty alike and had succeeded in simultaneously educating and entertaining viewers. A crowd favorite was the surprise ending entitled "My Best Friend" that was edited to overemphasize our comradery. The ending showcased Mr. Barndt and I embracing in slow motion, riding arm-in-arm down a two-person slide in tandem, smiling in slow motion as we gazed into each other's eyes while simultaneously holding our guts due to excruciating laughter, etc. as Queen's hit song, "You're My Best Friend" was being played in the background.

The two of us looked like we were transported directly from the 1970s, but we knew the students would be highly *EDUtained* with the end result, so we pressed onward.

One scene focused on me, grim-faced, completing several pull-ups on a monkey bar. As I was shown grunting with each pull-up, the camera panned downward to reveal Mr. Barndt supporting my legs and lifting me up with each heave (see Figure 13). The kids roared with laughter. When the movie was over, the crowd responded with thunderous applause. They wanted more!

Why bother?

Students enjoy seeing their teachers out of character and in a setting other than the classroom. Additionally, students pay attention when their leaders act silly. If an educator wants to teach students an important life skill like playground safety for example, showing students acceptable and unacceptable playground behaviors in a fun way will definitely hold student attention more than if the expectations were simply listed on a PowerPoint slide. All students need to be respectful, responsible, and safe on the playground.

Suggestions:

⇒ Don't film or do anything that you will regret.

⇒ Only wear school-appropriate attire.

⇒ Make sure the information that you want students to learn is the focus.

⇒ If you film outdoors, make sure the actors speak loudly or carry a mic.

The Skinny:

Act silly sometimes to build student rapport and create engaging opportunities to reinforce appropriate school-wide behaviors.

Figure 13: Funkadelic Athletic Swag

Chapter Fourteen

DMSCB

Does Mr. Svencer Chew Boogers?
-4th grade student

While walking past my classroom, a chant that can commonly be heard radiating out into the hallway while we are learning long division is as follows:

Divide.
Multiply.
Subtract.
Compare.
Bring Down.
Say it loud with a frown.

Students love the chant, embrace the chant, and remember the long division steps because of the chant. As an educator, I attempt to incorporate mnemonic devices as much as possible into my lessons. Furthermore, I encourage students to create their own mnemonic devices. Some of my favorite student-created mnemonic devices that relate to long division include:

- Does Mom Sell Cooked Boogers?
- Does Mr. Svencer Chuck Babies?
- Dancing Monsters Sure Can Boogie.
- Does Mother Sell Chopped Barf?
- Does Mom Sell Chunky Brains?

Students' mnemonic devices are not always school-appropriate when they first create them, but the devices can always be altered to be suitable for school.

Another mnemonic device that we use to help us remember what resources most plants need to make food is referred to as LAWN in my classroom. Most lawns contain grass, which is a type of plant, so the letters L A W N are appropriate. See example below:

Plants need...

Light
Air
Water
Nutrients

...to make their own food.

Because of the aforementioned mnemonic device, I have observed that students are able to remember what resources plants need to make food much easier than the students that did not utilize LAWN as a mnemonic device in prior years.

Why bother?

During my years as a teacher, I have found that the use of mnemonic devices is perhaps the most beneficial learning technique available to students. Mnemonic devices increase a student's efficiency in dedicating information to his/her long-term memory, which decreases wasted study time. It should also be noted, when students are given the opportunity to create their own mnemonic devices, the opportunity provides students with the skill set to create their own mnemonic devices for years to come. Lastly, as you've already read, mnemonic devices can be very *EDUtaining* for teachers and students alike (see Figure 14).

Suggestions:

⇒ Show students examples of mnemonic devices during the first week of school.
⇒ Give students time to create mnemonic devices of their own.

⇒ Create mnemonic devices for hard to learn information.

The Skinny:

Utilize mnemonic devices in your classroom to help students mentally organize newly learned information for quick retrieval in the future.

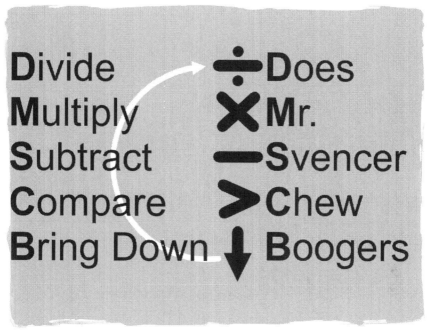

Figure 14: DMSCB

Chapter Fifteen

The Past

The pretzel dance is super fun!
-4th grade student

Incorporating stories from your past that relate directly to what students are learning can prove to be very *EDUtaining*. Because of my days as an (esteemed) pretzel maker at Auntie Anne's, when teaching a lesson on utilizing sequence words I was able to create an explanatory paragraph that described how to make a pretzel. My students' eyes were glued to the paragraph, because I prefaced the reading of the piece by telling students that I had previously worked at the famous pretzel store while in high school and college. Because of their acute attentiveness directed toward the paragraph, students had a heightened ability and motivation to discuss text features as well as identify the sequence words included within my sample essay.

The aforementioned activity was followed by an in-class assignment that required students to use sequence words to write an explanatory paragraph of their own. Moreover, it just so happened that DiscoSnack was scheduled for the same day. (If you are not familiar with DiscoSnack, please refer to chapter one.)

After students were finished writing their paragraphs, to transition into DiscoSnack, I described how I used to take it upon myself to perform a self-created pretzel dance as patrons passed by the store window. I shared how friends that worked my same shift would join in and perform the dance with me. I shared how the dance was so well received by the management at Auntie Anne's that I was given the privilege to represent the Auntie Anne's organization at a local elementary school by teaching the school's students how to perform the dance as well as how to make famous Auntie Anne's pretzels. (Clearly, I did not share the secret recipe.)

After sharing my dance story, DiscoSnack commenced, and I proceeded to show the students in my own class how to perform the pretzel dance that I had created while working at Auntie Anne's (see Figure 15). Of course, they loved the dance, and we all had a great time.

Tying in stories from my pretzel past helped me to build rapport with my students, held student interest, and assisted in creating a fun classroom environment. Incorporating movement between lessons via DiscoSnack was also a great way to help students release some of their energy.

> **Incorporating movement between lessons via DiscoSnack was also a great way to help students release some of their energy.**

On another occasion, when I was teaching a science lesson on electrical circuits, I discussed my first high school job as a game room attendant at Chuck E. Cheese. I explained how one particular wire inside a stubborn ski ball machine would repeatedly become detached and create a break in a circuit within the machine. I shared how the break in the circuit stopped the flow of electricity and frequently caused the machine to malfunction. I shared how I would have to re-attach the wire to complete the circuit and get the machine functioning properly again.

The students were engrossed into my story, because many could relate to my experience. Consequently, they gained a better understanding of how game machines at Chuck E. Cheese could malfunction. As chance would have it, we were also celebrating a birthday that day, so I proceeded to show students the Chuck E. Cheese "Happy Birthday" dance that I was required to perform while dressed in the Chuck E. Cheese rat costume that all workers had to take turns wearing. The students thought the dance was hysterical, and I had begun to regret ever showing them the dance in the first place.

Why bother?

Relating stories from your past to what students are learning helps draw their attention into the lesson and creates an opportunity for students to make a connection to what they are learning. As mentioned previously, sharing brief stories from your past also helps to build a positive rapport with students.

Suggestions:

⇒ Make certain that the stories being shared are appropriate to the age level and subject area being taught.

⇒ Never share stories that you don't want being shared at the dinner table that evening.

⇒ Keep the stories concise. The time spent on the stories being shared should never outlast the time spent on the actual concept being taught. (We've all experienced the substitute teachers that were notorious for going off on tangents that did not relate to what was to be the focus of the lesson. I'll admit, while in high school, I was one of those high school kids that attempted to get the substitutes off topic. Shame on me!)

The Skinny:

Share concise and school-appropriate stories from your past that relate directly to what is being taught to provide students with an engaging reference point from which they can mentally retrieve the information in the future.

Figure 15: The Pretzel Dance

Chapter Sixteen

The Parable

Can you tell us another story?
-4th grade student

As I was reading my Bible one evening, I became intrigued at how engaging Jesus' parables were. Jesus taught important lessons and truths via narratives to which people could easily relate. I figured, if the Creator of the Universe used parables, then parables must be effective. As a result of my thoughts, I decided to try the parable technique on my students.

About a week later, I reviewed the definitions of lines, line segments, rays, planes, and points via my own parable. I proceeded to incorporate the definitions of each aforementioned geometric term by drawing the accepted visual representations of the terms on my interactive whiteboard (see Figure 16) as I verbally integrated the term names as characters in my story. My narrative went something like this:

> Long ago, Line DE thought he was better than his line segments, because he could go on forever in both directions and see the world. He was never ending. The line segments began to feel worthless and sad, because they had a definite beginning and end. One day, a plane was catapulted off course and knocked a line segment out from within Line DE. Because of this catastrophe, Line DE was split into two and had become Ray DC and Ray EF. Line DE now felt disconnected, confused, and unwhole. Line DE realized the importance of line segments and apologized to the isolated line segment in order to hopefully feel whole again. Out of compassion, the line segment re-bridged the gap between Ray DC and Ray EF to make Line DE whole again. As time went by, the line segment that compassionately bridged the gap for Line DE began to boast about his importance in the

universe and made his points feel worthless. The line segment boasted that he held Line DE together. He made fun of all the points, because they had no length. Points were simply a location in space. As luck would have it, a plane got catapulted off course again and knocked a point out from within the boastful line segment, which split him into two separate line segments. Unsurprisingly, the boastful line segment felt disconnected, confused, and unwhole, which made Line DE feel the same way, as the boastful line segment was a part of Line DE. The boastful line segment wanted to feel whole again, so he promptly apologized to the isolated point. Because the point was compassionate, he re-bridged the gap between the two disconnected line segments to make both the boastful line segment and Line DE feel whole again. In the end, the line, line segment, and point learned that they all had a specific role in the universe and needed each other to function properly.

There may be some minor mathematical misconceptions in my story, but it served its purpose in meeting my objective of helping students review the definitions for lines, line segments, rays, points, and planes. In fact, immediately following the story, I asked students if my story helped them to review the aforementioned geometric terms. There was a unanimous show of hands in favor of the technique. They even asked if they could integrate mathematical concepts into stories of their own. Why not?

I figured, if the Creator of the Universe used parables, then parables must be effective.

Why bother?

Narratives that incorporate curriculum-based terms and concepts beyond the main story line both educate and entertain a child. People love stories. If a teacher can incorporate a newly learned concept into a cohesive story, the benefits will be amazing. Narratives are very engaging and create a timeline to help the mind organize information more easily than if someone simply tried memorizing the included academic information separately. When new concepts are included within a narrative, they become part of a whole that students can reflect upon.

Suggestions:

⇒ Revisit memorable parables and narratives from your past to familiarize your mind with their effective format. Most engaging stories contain a conflict, plot events, and a resolution.

⇒ Even if you are not a great storyteller, give it a try. You may be pleasantly surprised.

⇒ If you don't have any success making up stories of your own, give students the opportunity to create stories that incorporate terms related to what you are teaching. Give students time to share their stories with the class. The world is full of great storytellers. Over time, you will collect a bunch of stories that can be reused for years to come. If you don't have enough class time in your day to allow for students to create stories, assign the stories as homework or extra credit.

The Skinny:

Embed important concepts within short narratives when introducing or reviewing new material.

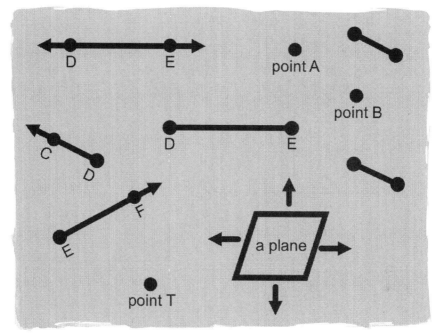

Figure 16: The Parable

Chapter Seventeen

Music Videos

Can we watch the domino video again?
-4th grade student

During my first year of marriage, I was helping my wife baby-sit a house and dog for my brother-in-law and sister-in-law, Greg and Sherry. During that time, I happened to be watching the VH1 Top 20 Video Countdown on Sherry and Greg's television one Saturday morning. I was blown away by the intricate and synchronized dance moves performed by the band OK Go in a music video for their song "Here It Goes Again." The band bounced around like robotic marionettes while humbly flaunting an impressive choreographed dance routine performed atop eight powered-up treadmills. The band's video went on to win a Grammy Award[1] for "Best Short-Form Music Video" in 2007, and the video has millions of views on YouTube.[2] Needless to say, I was highly entertained, and much of the world was as well.

A few years later, OK Go teamed up with State Farm and Synn Labs to create a unique music video entitled "This Too Shall Pass – Rube Goldberg Machine version."[3] The video showcases a continuous chain reaction of interconnected simple machines and inanimate objects synchronized to the band's song "This Too Shall Pass." The chain reaction occurs for almost four minutes while the band members move about and lip-sync the lyrics. Toy cars roll down inclined planes. A metal basket attached to a string wraps around a screw. Weighted pulley systems trigger levers and gears. Pianos are destroyed. Vintage televisions are shattered. Dominoes fall. And, among other things, the band members have paint shot at them from cannons. OK Go literally looked like they got into a fight with a bunch of Skittles. To give you a better image of the video, envision the board game Mouse Trap with superpowers.

Due to the video's advanced scientific content, it can easily be incorporated into a physics lesson. I personally chose to show my students the video at the end of a science unit I taught on simple machines. We watched the video two times. The first time we watched for pleasure (see Figure 17). The second time, students had to identify all of the simple machines included in the video and discuss how each simple machine worked. We had a blast! (Needless to say, we actually ended up watching the video more than twice.) Moreover, the video allowed students to observe how science can be utilized in entertaining ways in the real world.

Like "Here It Goes Again," the Rube Goldberg version of "This Too Shall Pass" has millions of views on YouTube. The numbers speak for themselves. If millions of people find the video engaging, it is likely students will as well!

To hold fans over as they anxiously awaited the release of the Rube Goldberg version of "This Too Shall Pass," OK Go filmed another video for the song that featured the Notre Dame marching band and a children's choir.[4] The video was filmed and recorded live in a grassy field with the four original OK Go band members dressed in marching band uniforms. The original members of OK Go play an accordion, snare drum, bass drum, and xylophone throughout the video. Unexpectedly, however, members of the Notre Dame marching band randomly "pop up" out of the grassy field dressed in military-grade camouflage body suits and begin to play their previously concealed instruments along with OK Go. (My students refer to the camouflaged marching band members as creepers.)

OK Go literally looked like they got into a fight with a bunch of *Skittles*.

During a science lesson on animal adaptations, I showed my students the aforementioned video to help illustrate how effective camouflage can be in making animals or humans almost invisible to predators. The video provided students with a highly *EDUtaining* visual of camouflage in action.

Once again, a couple more years later, OK Go teamed up with Chevy to create yet another music video that involved science. Only this time, part of the video was broadcasted via a Chevy ad during Super Bowl XLVI, which helped the music video go viral. Below is the description OK Go included with the video/ad for their song "Needing/Getting" when they posted it on YouTube:

> ...OK Go set up over 1000 instruments over two miles of desert outside Los Angeles. A Chevy Sonic was outfitted with retractable pneumatic arms designed to play the instruments, and the band recorded...Needing/Getting, singing as they played the instrument array with the car. The video took 4 months of preparation and 4 days of shooting and recording. There are no ringers or stand-ins; Damian [lead vocals and guitar] took stunt driving lessons. Each piano had the lowest octaves tuned to the same note so that they'd play the right note no matter where they were struck...[5]

As you have just read, the music video/ad for "Needing/Getting" has physics concepts written all over it.

If you haven't already took notice, many of OK Go's music videos tend to rank highly in *EDUtaining* students as well as the general public. However, don't limit yourself to using solely OK Go music videos. The truth is, the aforementioned videos may not apply to what you teach. As you will read in the suggestions section of this chapter, other artists' music videos can be used in the classroom as well.

Why bother?

Incorporating music videos that relate to your school's curriculum will enhance instruction, engage students, spur valuable discussion, and assist students in making associations to what is being taught. Directors, editors, musicians, actors, and producers spend a lot of time, energy, and money creating cohesive and entertaining music videos. If you happen to stumble upon a school-appropriate video that relates to what you are teaching, use it! Someone else did all of the *EDUtaining* work for you! All you have to do is hit play, sit back, and enjoy!

Suggestions:

⇒ Turn on the VH1 Top 20 Video Countdown as you are completing chores around the house on a Saturday morning. An *EDUtaining* video may present itself.

⇒ Record the VH1 Top 20 Video Countdown or similar music video broadcast, and fast forward through the broadcast to scan for possible music videos that can be utilized in your classroom.

⇒ As you take notice of the radio while driving, listen for songs with school-appropriate content. Search for the school-appropriate songs on YouTube to find out if any of the corresponding music videos can be incorporated into your curriculum.

⇒ Many music videos present a strong story structure that include main characters, a setting, a conflict, plot events, and a resolution. If you teach story structure, have students fill in a story map as they view a popular music video that contains an obvious story line. Taylor Swift has a variety of music videos with strong story structure.

⇒ If you teach a psychology course on conditioning, OK Go's official video for their song "White Knuckles" shows the band members using stimuli to get a bunch of canines to perform numerous tricks in unison with the music (OK Go Again).[6]

⇒ If you teach a lesson on American Civil Rights or the United States Constitution, Switchfoot's official music video for "The Sound (John M. Perkins' Blues)" features words from American civil rights activist John M. Perkins interspersed with civil rights protest footage and marches from the past.[7] The video also includes the opening line from the Preamble to the U.S. Constitution in addition to John M. Perkins' thought provoking quote, "Love is the final fight." You can discuss the meaning of Perkins' quote and how it compares to the teachings of Dr. Martin Luther King, Jr.

⇒ If you teach stop motion animation, Switchfoot's official music video for "Awakening" showcases the technique using paper.[8]

⇒ If you can't access YouTube or similar sites from school, many videos can be purchased and downloaded at home from sites like iTunes or Amazon and brought to school via a data storage device.

⇒ Sites like keepvid.com allow videos from YouTube to be downloaded free of charge for personal use. Furthermore, some web browsers like Mozilla Firefox allow users to download a free extension called DownloadHelper, which, like keepvid.com, permits users to download and store YouTube videos for personal use.

The Skinny:

Incorporate music videos that relate to your school's curriculum to enhance instruction, engage students, spur discussion, and build rapport.

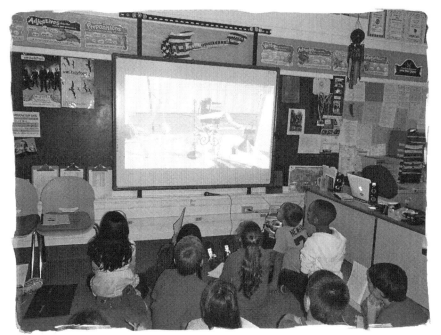

Figure 17: Students viewing "This Too Shall Pass – Rube Goldberg Machine version"

Conclusion

Because the world is changing at a rapid and accelerating pace, those who are unwilling or unable to take risks will become ineffective if not obsolete.[1]

-Jim McCormick, *professional skydiver & innovator*

One Friday afternoon, I was standing outside of the school entrance with a couple of my male colleagues (referred to as brothas' to one another) after dismissal, and we were palling around as usual. As we were discussing my permission to allow several students to throw snowballs at a random pair of shoes hanging from a tree on the playground during extra recess, one of my brothas' made a remark that stuck with me over the years. He stated, "One day, we're gonna' look back and say, Svencer has been doing this [illustrious] stuff for years."

What he was saying was that some of my judgments and techniques might not be common practice, but they certainly don't undermine or hinder a child's education. Instead they enhance, engage, and/or bring joy to a student's education. For instance, to some, allowing a student to throw snowballs at a pair of shoes (with intent to knock them down) hanging from a tree on the school playground may not be deemed appropriate. However, if one would take a minute and contemplate the idea, he/she would come to the realization that throwing snowballs at a pair of shoes in a tree (positioned far from students playing, a school window, or classroom) will do no more than bring joy to a student.

It is my hope that the ideas in this book will act as a catalyst for all educators, prospective, past, and present, to evaluate what they do and do not allow or deem appropriate in a school setting. They must ask themselves if some of the rules are based upon old and irrelevant standards, or if there is area for change and improvement in a postmodern educational setting? Ultimately, the decision is up to the teacher, and all decisions should be respected. It is my hope that genuine reflection would be applied to what educators deem as effective, ineffective, safe, unsafe, appropriate, or inappropriate in a school setting. A good teacher should never hold on to an irrelevant rule out of stubbornness but be able to justify why he/she supports "said" rule, much like every teacher is expected to be able to justify what he/she is teaching based upon state-mandated academic standards.

On another note, I am very grateful to be given the opportunity to share the ideas and techniques included in this book. I have found the ideas in this nonfiction text to bring so much life and excitement into my classroom and school. The ideas in this book keep my classroom relevant. I love my job and feel so blessed to work with a supportive administration and staff that fosters a fun and *EDUtaining* environment that allows for *EDUtaining* incentives and techniques to be used. In fact, every faculty and staff member at my school, including my principal, has *EDUtaining* techniques of his/her own and embrace at least some aspects of *EDUtainment* as well. For that I am grateful. If you are reading this book, it is my desire that you will embrace the ideas of *EDUtainment* and hopefully incorporate this philosophy into your ever-changing postmodern classroom.

NOTES

Introduction

1. McCormick, J. (2009). You want me to do what? - risking to win. Retrieved October 5, 2012, from http://www.takerisks.com/inspirationalstoriesarticle.html

Chapter 3: Rock N' Rules

1. DiBiase, J. (2000, September 25). Switchfoot learns to breathe [An Interview with Jon Foreman]. *JFH*.

Chapter 10: Hoop Dreams

1. Scheerer, L. (2005, August). Beach balls and cowboy hats encourage participation. *East Penn Chronicle*.

Chapter 11: Karaoke Choreography

1. Scholastic. (2010). Sing Karaoke, "Types of Lines," Retrieved October 5, 2012 from http://studyjams.scholastic.com/studyjams/jams/math/geometry/types-of-lines.htm
2. Campbell, K. (2009, March 5). Thank you. [Personal email].

Chapter 17: Music Videos

1. The Recoding Academy. (2006). 49th Annual Grammy Awards Winners List. Retrieved October 7, 2012, from http://www.grammy.com/nominees/search?artist=&title=&year=2006&genre=All
2. emimusic. (2009, February 26). *OK Go – Here It Goes Again.* Retrieved October 7, 2012, from http://www.youtube.com/watch?v=dTAAsCNK7RA
3. OkGo. (2010, March 1). *OK Go – This Too Shall Pass – Rube Goldberg Machine version – Official.* Retrieved October 7, 2012, from http://www.youtube.com/watch?v=qybUFnY7Y8w
4. OkGo. (2010, January 8). *OK Go – This Too Shall Pass – Official Video.* Retrieved October 5, 2012, from http://www.youtube.com/watch?v=UJKythlXAIY
5. OkGo. (2012, February 5). *OK Go - Needing/Getting – Official Video.* Retrieved October 5, 2012, from www.youtube.com/watch?v=

MejbOFk7H6c

6. OkGo. (2010, September 19). *OK Go – White Knuckles – Official Video*. Retrieved October 7, 2012, from http://www.youtube.com/watch?v=nHlJODYBLKs
7. Switchfoot. (2010, June 16). *Switchfoot – The Sound (John M. Perkins' Blues)*. Retrieved October 7, 2012, from http://www.youtube.com/watch?v=mNQgABsUfK8
8. SwitchfootVEVO. (2009, November 7). *Switchfoot – Awakening*. Retrieved, October 7, 2012, from http://www.youtube.com/watch?v=cl64-XHE7zo

Conclusion

1. McCormick, J. (2009). You want me to do what? - risking to win. Retrieved October 5, 2012, from http://www.takerisks.com/inspirationalstoriesarticle.html

Acknowledgements

I have many people I'd like to thank for helping me with this book:

* The great Teacher and Redeemer of the World written about in the four gospels of the Bible, for blessing me with the ability and opportunity to write this book as well as teach students. You are my hero.

* My patient wife and helper, Tina, for encouraging me, being my sounding board, and believing in me throughout this process.

* My Mom and Dad, for loving, raising, and making many sacrifices for me.

* My sis, for being a great sister. Your heart for others inspires me.

* Grandma, for being the first to read the introduction to this book and responding with kind comments and words of encouragement.

* Jennifer Sheehan, for generously helping with editing numerous times. You are very talented.

* Christopher Elson, for providing the costume cover photo.

* Dr. Anthony at Millersville University, for introducing me to the Montessori methods. The Montessori methods, though different from my own, encouraged me to try new techniques, take risks, and find my niche in teaching.

* Heather and Alma, for mentoring me and guiding me during my first year as a teacher. Your mentorships were and still are invaluable to my career.

* Lexi, for being a knowledgeable team buddy with awesome ideas.

* Doug, for having unprecedented funkadelic athletic swagger.

* Chase, for coming up with the term "zombieing" and being a great disc golf brotha.

(continued)

(continued from previous)

* Brian Gingrich, for your willingness to answer all of my students' questions.

* Kliney and Maley, for being great directors, writers, filmers, producers, and editors of the playground safety video.

* Ira Schneider and Ron Hamsher, for making my student teaching experience successful.

* Kristen Campbell, for hiring me to work at Lincoln and supporting me in my nontraditional techniques. You are a great leader.

* Dr. A, for also embracing my unconventional methods.

* Grandma, Grandpap, Gams, and Pap for spending lots of quality time with me on the weekends as a child. You provided me with a lot of great memories! I'll never forgot camping and cleaning the bank late at night! You were some of my first *EDUtainers*. Thank you, Grandpap, for showing me how to work hard and stay organized.

* Bill Strickland, for providing direction during the early stages of this book.

* The Fishers, for cheering me on my first year of teaching and beyond!

* The Pukanecz Family, for giving me a funny story to tell!

* Lincoln Elementary Faculty and Staff, for putting up with my antics.

* My talented students and their loving parents.

* Jon, Tim, Chad, Romey, & Drew for being the most gracious band in the world!

Lastly, thank you to the countless others that have provided me with valuable information related to the publishing process.

About the Author

Bryan D. Svencer is a 4th grade teacher at Lincoln Elementary within the East Penn School District in Emmaus, PA, where he has been practicing his *EDUtainment* philosophy since 2005. Over and over again, he has been told, "You make learning fun!" One student told him, "If you were a hotel, you'd be 5 stars." Another wrote, "You are the best thing that ever happened to me." In 2008, Mr. Svencer received his Master of Science in Education degree from Wilkes University. In 2009, the Commonwealth of Pennsylvania recognized Mr. Svencer as a Keystone Technology Integrator for his exemplary integration of technology in the practice of teaching.

For fun, Mr. Svencer enjoys teaching, reading, riding waves, watching movies, serving the youth at his church, listening to lots of music, spending time with his family/friends, "frolfing," and partying with rock stars (see Chapter Three). He resides in Macungie, PA with his wife, Tina, and their daughter, Evangeline Grace.

Author's Sites
& Additional Resources:

www.YouTube.com/EDUtainment23

www.facebook.com/EDUtainment23

www.eastpennsd.org/teacherpages/bsvencer

Bryan D. Svencer, M.Ed.

EDUtainment: Entertainment in the K-12 Classroom

paperback | eBook